T0132025

The Big
BAD TRUCK

In Honor of Houston McKell III

Keyaira McKell and Houston McKell IV

Dedicated to our Mother
Leona (Newson) McKell
And our Grandmother
Eula McKell

INTRODUCTION

On February 14, 2019 our father (Houston III) passed away when my brother, Houston IV, and I were only 15 and 13 years old. He was a Navy Seal veteran, very hardworking & family-oriented man with an exuberant soul, the best father we could ever have, and more. As a tribute, we wrote poems and a short story to send him off with our love. Our grandmother was touched by our words and thought it was the perfect way to honor her son/our father, so she made sure to do everything she could to get our stories turned into a book that can not only be a souvenir to our family, but also comfort and inspire other grieving children and families all over the world—especially during the trying times of the COVID-19 pandemic, whose effects are still being felt by many. All we can do is help each other heal and inspire one another to keep hope, gratitude, patience, and love in our hearts in the midst of all the losses, fears, uncertainties, concerns, & doubts. This too shall pass!

Death of My Father

by Houston McKell IV

One day it will be everyone's turn to go.

But only God will know.

Until then, we serve on Earth;

For every sad death there will be a

Beautiful birth.

We're mourning a death

But there will be celebration and mirth.

Afterwards we'll go back

To our separate ways

But never forget this date.

Just sit back and count the days.

Thinking about the sorrow will only put you down.

Never feel sorrow because of a death, never frown;

God will not let you down.

Death will only make you stronger.

The Big Bad Truck

In Honor of Houston McKell III

Written and Illustrated By Keyaira McKell

Imagine a truck. One of those big, bad trucks.
A truck that could straight up look a blizzard in the eye
and drive through rain and snow like it ain't nothing
because it has four wheel drive.

I'm talking about a specific truck, though,
and this one didn't have a big brand name.
But that made no difference
because he could still do the same.

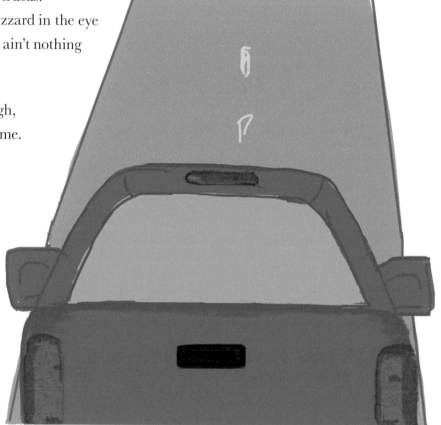

This truck was reckless in two ways:

The first one, because he purposely hit potholes and speed bumps;
ran red lights & stop signs.
He would go 80 miles per hour when the speed limit was 25.
And it was all for the thrill of it.
You would've thought he did professional stunts.

The second reason this truck was reckless was because he never wrecked.
Potholes, speed bumps, and other roadblocks were in the way,
but this truck was no joke.
That's why he was able to play around so much and only come out with a small scratch.
Because potholes, speed bumps, speed limits, stop signs, and red lights,
to this truck, were no match.

Psalms 23:4-"Even though I walk through the valley of the shadow of death, I will fear no evil, for you are
with me; your rod and your staff, they comfort me."

Now he played rough for a while. Running the streets all over town.

But after all the constant on-the-go, the truck started to slow down.

He noticed that he would soon run out of gas.

So he took a break from always going fast.

At this point he decided he could carry passengers, so he told everybody to 'Get in!'

He picked up new passengers at every stop; and if there was no more room they would just have to lap up.

The passengers were down to ride, they didn't hesitate to get inside.

They were ready to go all of the different ways and find out how this truck would drive them crazy.

Having a load to share the journey with made the truck feel proud.

So he filled his tank back up and turned the radio up loud.

Once again, the truck was back out on the streets.

But this time he didn't do the same stunts he used to do.

Well, he did…but not as rough.

He knew he was carrying passengers now,
so his focus became getting them to
their destination safely
and making sure they enjoyed the ride.

One of them needed a potty break?

He'd pull to the side.

One of them started to get hungry?

They stopped to get food.

One of them wanted to learn how to drive?

He'd let them take the wheel and teach them how to run the streets just as rough as he used to.

In return for the favors, they tried to keep the truck's interior clean
and offered gas money out of thanks.
The truck was so honored to be carrying the passengers
that he told them to put their money away.
And he let them go ahead and make messes on his floors,
press his buttons, and slam his doors.
He didn't mind driving them back and forth either, no matter
how much the mileage ran up and the gas tank ran down.

As years and years passed,
the truck's tires started losing air;
small cracks were appearing in the windshield;
and there was visible wear-and-tear.
His paint was fading and his brakes were gone.
The engine didn't start like it used to, either.
His energetic roar became an exhausted groan.

Going 80 when the speed limit was 25
became going 25 when the speed limit was 25— 40 every now and then.
60 if he really felt like doing something.

It's hard to believe, but this truck that used to do so much
now stayed in and out of the shop.
Couldn't even leave the driveway some days.
And worst of all, he had to start dropping off his passengers.
He was aware of his exhaustion
and he knew that there were many mechanics out there,
but none of their work would do.
He was ready to go to the junkyard, so that his worn out pieces
could be made into something new.

But there was a particular mechanic
that could fill back up the tires and the tank,
fix all the small cracks,
make the engine roar again,
and restore the truck completely.
Inside and out.

So, when the truck finally got an appointment with this mechanic
he rolled in with no doubt.

Psalms 30:5 - "Weeping may endure for a night, but joy cometh in the morning:'

This is the story of Houston McKell III.

His character could be told in similarity to a big, bad truck imagined on one heck of a journey (through life). Having a big, bad truck makes you feel better because it's dependable and strong. You know that you can weather a storm with a big, bad truck and he was that truck to the people that knew him. The embodiment of Houston as a truck also captures his go-getter mentality. Being so ready to get out on the road doesn't come easy. There are many bumps and blockages along the way to shake up the journey, but he wasn't one to back down from a challenge. He'd go in head first, ready to face whatever lay on the path in front of him and embraced the obstacles that marked the journey behind him. In 2008, Houston found out that his kidneys were failing along with other health complications and was told to only have a few months to live. This was one of the big obstacles that people would have expected to take a toll on his life 'in the fast lane' but that did not stop him. He persevered as 'the big, bad truck' steadily carrying on everyday and performing well as if nothing ever happened, leading him to enjoy one of the many delights of his journey, which were the adventures with his "Precious Cargo" (kids, family, & friends). They made the journey more worthwhile for him, as he did for them. Lamentably, Houston reached the end of the road, but his legacy carries on with his loved ones as they remember the joy of his presence and the good times they shared.

Word from Grandma
Ms. Eula McKell

Their dad's journey started over 50 years ago.
He started going Fast as he could.
Never took command
very well, he enjoyed having
control.
He was very smart/a genius
and kept everyone laughing.
This was his personality and
We loved him very much.

This Big Bad Truck
Houston McKell III
Was someone special
Because: "God Don't Make No Junk!"

The End

The Big Bad Truck
IN HONOR OF HOUSTON MCKELL III

Copyright © 2022 Keyaira McKell and Houston McKell IV.

All rights reserved. No part of this book may be used or reproduced by any means, graphic, electronic, or mechanical, including photocopying, recording, taping or by any information storage retrieval system without the written permission of the author except in the case of brief quotations embodied in critical articles and reviews.

iUniverse books may be ordered through booksellers or by contacting:

iUniverse
1663 Liberty Drive
Bloomington, IN 47403
www.iuniverse.com
844-349-9409

Because of the dynamic nature of the Internet, any web addresses or links contained in this book may have changed since publication and may no longer be valid. The views expressed in this work are solely those of the author and do not necessarily reflect the views of the publisher, and the publisher hereby disclaims any responsibility for them.

Any people depicted in stock imagery provided by Getty Images are models, and such images are being used for illustrative purposes only. Certain stock imagery © Getty Images.

NIV
Scripture quotations marked NIV are taken from the Holy Bible, New International Version®. NIV®. Copyright © 1973, 1978, 1984 by International Bible Society. Used by permission of Zondervan. All rights reserved. [Biblica]

ISBN: 978-1-6632-4486-4 (sc)
ISBN: 978-1-6632-4485-7 (e)

Library of Congress Control Number: 2022916177

Print information available on the last page.

iUniverse rev. date: 10/04/2022

Printed in the United States
by Baker & Taylor Publisher Services